What Makes a Reptile a Reptile?

A Bucky and Bingo Learning Adventure

WITH BUCKY AND BINGO

Andi Cann

I hope you enjoy learning about reptiles today! Please visit my website https://www.andicann.com and register your email address. You will receive a free book and be the first to know about new books, special offers, and free stuff!

If you have a chance, please write a review. It helps other readers and me, an independent author. Thank you!

Andi

A note to readers.

Snakes, lizards, geckos, iguanas, even turtles are curiosities that fascinate everyone, especially children! Some fun facts about reptiles include:

1. They evolved from amphibians! (Although amphibians still exist.)

2. There are 8000 species of reptiles.

3. Reptiles don't live on Antarctica because they are ectothermic (they only get their body warmed from outside sources.) But they do live on every other continent.

4. Reptiles are one of the oldest species on the planet. Some sources think turtles have been here for 200 million years.

5. Only 2% of all snakes are venomous. More people die from bee stings than snake bites!

6. Some lizards lose their tail to escape but then grow a new one.

7. Reptiles cannot smell through their nose. Instead, they "smell" by flicking their tongue and collecting scent particles. They use a type of internal database (a special organ) to determine the scent. Isn't that cool?

Have a great time learning about lizards and other reptiles. Before long, you will be a junior herpetologist!

For all parents who support their children's love of reading and reptiles!

Hi! I'm Bucky. Today we saw a snake! It was a little bit creepy. I asked my parents, "What kind of animal is a snake?"

They answered a snake is a reptile. "Huh? What's a reptile? What kinds of animals are reptiles?"

When I opened the magic mystery book about nature, it showed me a picture of a horn.

The book asked, "Do you know what a horn and a snake have in common? I looked up and shrugged. I didn't know.

The book said, "Keratin!"

Reptiles are the only creatures whose skin is keratin. Keratin is a dry, scaly substance that allows reptiles to feel through their skin. Their skin is super hard and yet, sensitive, too!

Reptiles also have cold blood. What does that mean? It means they feel warm when it's warm outside and cold when it's cold. Because they can control their body temperature, they can exist in many climates.

Wouldn't it be weird if you could control your body temperature?

Brrr....I would feel like an ice cube. I like being warm-blooded. Thank you very much!

Two other things make a reptile a reptile. They have four legs (most of the time), and they lay eggs.

But wait a minute! Bingo has four legs, and he's not a reptile.

And snakes have NO legs. The book says there are exceptions. Whatever that means!

But what about the fact that they lay eggs? Birds lay eggs. They're not reptiles.

Bingo and I talked with Lucy and looked at the book again. Lucy said, "Reptiles must have all four of those things. Four legs (tetrapods- unless a snake), lay eggs, be cold-blooded,

AND have scales and no hair or fur. So, remember the word SCALE.

S = Scales

C= Cold-blooded

A=

Animal

L= Legs

E= Eggs

So whenever you meet a new animal, and you want to know what it is, ask yourself:

Does it have scales?

Is it cold-blooded?

Is it an animal?

Does it have legs?

Does it lay eggs?

Let's try it out!

Here is an owl. It lays eggs and is an animal. But, it only has two legs, does not have scales, and is not cold-blooded. So it is NOT a reptile.

What about this lizard? Scales? Check.

Cold-blooded? Check.

Four legs? Check

Animal? Check.

Lays eggs? Check.

This lizard IS a reptile!

What about this turtle? Is it a reptile? It has scales, is cold-blooded, has four feet, and lays eggs. Yes, a turtle is a reptile!

What about this creature? It has scales. It's cold-blooded, and it lays eggs. But…no feet. This FISH is NOT a reptile!

What's that, Bingo? Is a frog a reptile? Let's take a look. They are cold-blooded. They have four legs. They lay eggs. BUT they don't have scaly skin. So, frogs are not reptiles.

We checked an
iguana,

colorful chameleons, and a crocodile. Yes. They are all reptiles.

I don't know about you, Bingo, but reptiles look a little creepy. And, Mom said some of them bite! OUCH! I don't want to get too close. But I like knowing what makes a reptile a reptile. Don't you?

Reptiles, in order of appearance:

There are many other books by Andi Cann. Check them out at your favorite book seller!

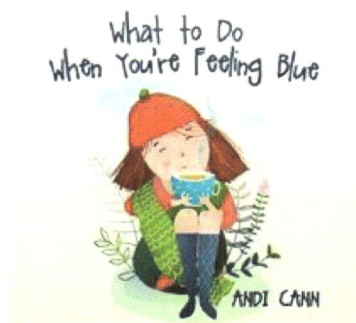
What to Do When You're Feeling Blue
ANDI CANN

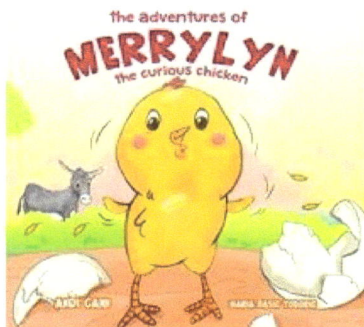
the adventures of MERRYLYN the curious chicken

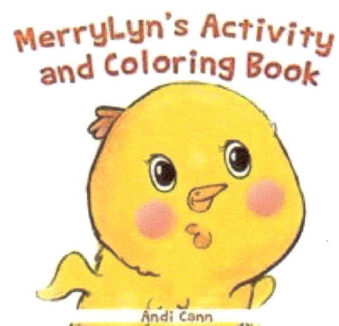
MerryLyn's Activity and Coloring Book
Andi Cann

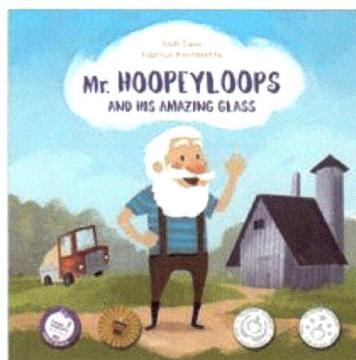
Mr. HOOPEYLOOPS AND HIS AMAZING GLASS

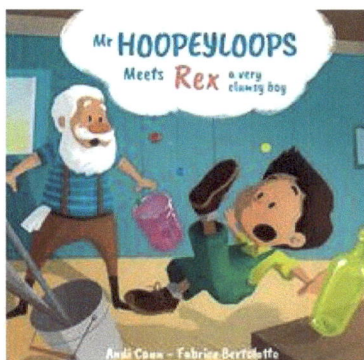
Mr HOOPEYLOOPS Meets Rex a very clumsy boy
Andi Cann - Fabrice Bertolotto

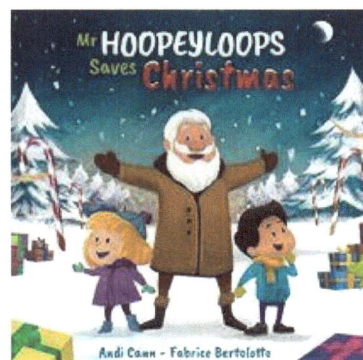
Mr HOOPEYLOOPS Saves Christmas
Andi Cann - Fabrice Bertolotto

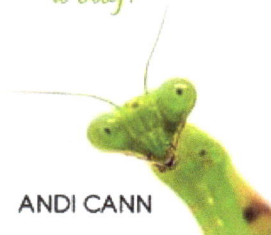
What makes a bug a bug?
ANDI CANN

What makes a bird a bird?
ANDI CANN

What makes a mammal a mammal?
ANDI CANN

Published by MindView Press: Hibou

ISBN-13:   978-1-949761-37-5   eBook

ISBN-13:   978-1-949761-38-2   Paperback

Thank you for reading!

www.ingramcontent.com/pod-product-compliance
Lightning Source LLC
Chambersburg PA
CBHW041240020426

42333CB00002B/35